EARTH'S ENERGY EXPERIMENTS

OIL ENERGY PROJECTS

Easy Energy Activities for
Future Engineers!

MEGAN BORGERT-SPANIOL

CONSULTING EDITOR, DIANE CRAIG, M.A./READING SPECIALIST

Super Sandcastle

An Imprint of Abdo Publishing
abdopublishing.com

abdopublishing.com

Published by Abdo Publishing, a division of ABDO, PO Box 398166, Minneapolis, Minnesota 55439. Copyright © 2019 by Abdo Consulting Group, Inc. International copyrights reserved in all countries. No part of this book may be reproduced in any form without written permission from the publisher. Super SandCastle™ is a trademark and logo of Abdo Publishing.

Printed in the United States of America, North Mankato, Minnesota
052018
092018

THIS BOOK CONTAINS RECYCLED MATERIALS

Design and Production: Mighty Media, Inc.
Editor: Liz Salzmann
Cover Photographs: iStockphoto; Mighty Media, Inc.
Interior Photographs: iStockphoto; Mighty Media, Inc.; Shutterstock; Wikimedia Commons

The following manufacturers/names appearing in this book are trademarks: Anderson's, Dawn®, Hershey's®, Karo®, Pillsbury Creamy Supreme®, Pyrex®, Reynolds®, Swedish Fish®, Walgreens

Library of Congress Control Number: 2017961710

Publisher's Cataloging-in-Publication Data

Names: Borgert-Spaniol, Megan, author.
Title: Oil energy projects: Easy energy activities for future engineers! / by Megan Borgert-Spaniol.
Other titles: Easy energy activities for future engineers!
Description: Minneapolis, Minnesota : Abdo Publishing, 2019. | Series: Earth's energy experiments
Identifiers: ISBN 9781532115646 (lib.bdg.) | ISBN 9781532156366 (ebook)
Subjects: LCSH: Petroleum as fuel--Juvenile literature. | Handicraft--Juvenile literature. | Science projects--Juvenile literature. | Earth sciences--Experiments--Juvenile literature.
Classification: DDC 553.28--dc23

Super SandCastle™ books are created by a team of professional educators, reading specialists, and content developers around five essential components—phonemic awareness, phonics, vocabulary, text comprehension, and fluency—to assist young readers as they develop reading skills and strategies and increase their general knowledge. All books are written, reviewed, and leveled for guided reading and early reading intervention programs for use in shared, guided, and independent reading and writing activities to support a balanced approach to literacy instruction.

TO ADULT HELPERS

The projects in this title are fun and simple. There are just a few things to remember to keep kids safe. Some projects require the use of sharp or hot objects. Also, kids may be using messy materials such as glue or paint. Make sure they protect their clothes and work surfaces. Review the projects before starting, and be ready to assist when necessary.

KEY SYMBOLS

Watch for these warning symbols in this book. Here is what they mean.

HOT!
You will be working with something hot. Get help!

SHARP!
You will be working with a sharp object. Get help!

CONTENTS

WHAT IS OIL ENERGY?

Oil energy is created by burning oil. Oil is a black liquid found underground. It is a **fossil fuel**. Oil forms from the remains of ancient plants and animals. The process takes millions of years.

CRUDE OIL

Humans pump crude oil to Earth's surface. Then the oil is processed into different products. These are called **petroleum** products. They have many different uses.

OIL REFINERY

Oil is a nonrenewable **resource**. This is because it takes so long for new oil to form. It's possible that we could use it up. Some experts say Earth's oil supply could be gone in 50 years.

OIL WELL

OIL WELLS TO REFINERIES

Scientists help locate oil **reservoirs** in underground rock. Then workers drill wells into the reservoirs. The oil wells pump crude oil to the surface. The oil is sent to **refineries**. Refineries turn the oil into usable products.

OFFSHORE DRILLING

Some oil reservoirs are underneath lake and ocean floors. Offshore oil rigs are used to drill into these reservoirs. Some of these structures are very large. Rigs that are far from shore have living quarters for the crew.

OIL TANKERS

Some oil is shipped to **refineries** in large oil tankers. Tankers can also carry oil products such as gasoline from refineries. They take the gasoline to countries that don't make enough of their own.

OIL PIPELINES

Pipelines are another way oil is taken to and from refineries. Oil pipelines can be above ground or underground. Oil pipelines are the least expensive way to move oil long distances.

OIL ENERGY HISTORY

Oil has been used for thousands of years. Ancient people used the **petroleum** product bitumen as a building material. They also burned oil for heat and to use as a weapon.

The first modern oil **refineries** were built in the 1850s. These refineries made oil products used for lighting and **lubrication**.

Today, most oil is used to make fuels that are burned for power. Some fuels power cars or machines. Others heat buildings or produce electricity at power plants.

OIL LANTERN

EDWIN DRAKE

Edwin Drake was born in 1819 in Greenville, New York. In 1857, the Seneca Oil Company hired him to get oil from a natural oil seep in Titusville, Pennsylvania. Drake dug a well deep into the ground. In 1859, Drake struck oil in Titusville. He had built the first successful oil well in the United States!

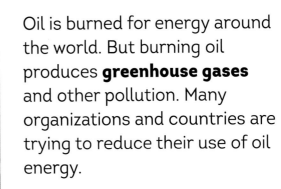

GAS STATION

Oil is burned for energy around the world. But burning oil produces **greenhouse gases** and other pollution. Many organizations and countries are trying to reduce their use of oil energy.

MATERIALS

Here are some of the materials that you will need for the projects in this book.

BASTER

CLEAR JAR

CLEAR NARROW VASE

COCOA POWDER

CORN SYRUP

COTTON BALLS

CUPCAKE PAN

FOIL CUPCAKE LINERS

FOOD COLORING

FROSTING

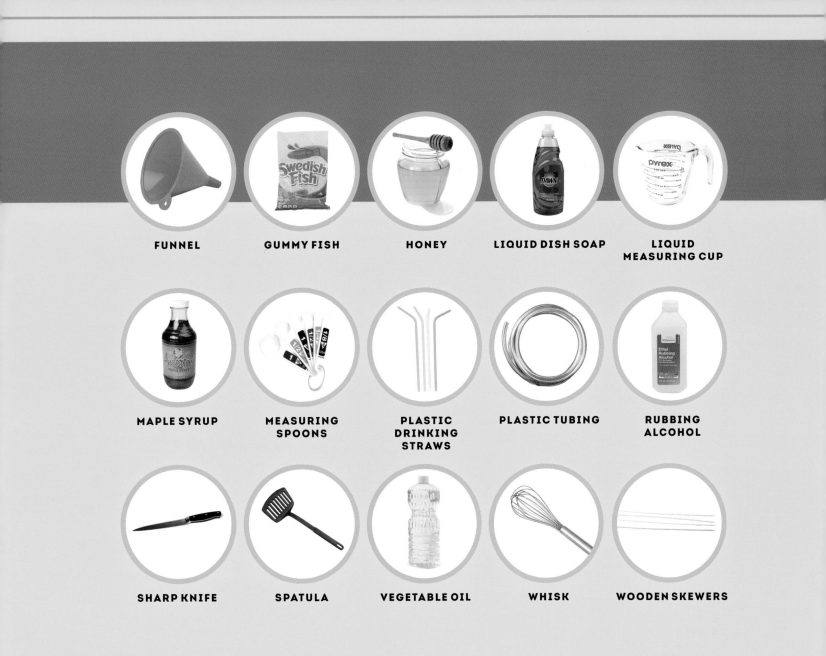

FUNNEL

GUMMY FISH

HONEY

LIQUID DISH SOAP

LIQUID MEASURING CUP

MAPLE SYRUP

MEASURING SPOONS

PLASTIC DRINKING STRAWS

PLASTIC TUBING

RUBBING ALCOHOL

SHARP KNIFE

SPATULA

VEGETABLE OIL

WHISK

WOODEN SKEWERS

OIL FORMATION SANDWICH

MATERIALS: white, rye & wheat bread (1 slice each), paper towels, gummy fish, books, sharp knife

Oil forms from the remains of sea plants and animals. Over time, these remains get buried under layers of sand, rock, and soil. Heat and pressure slowly turn the remains into oil. This process takes millions of years!

1. Carefully tear the crusts off each slice of bread.

2. Place the white bread on a paper towel. Place a gummy fish on the bread.

3. Place the rye bread on the white bread. Place three gummy fish on the rye bread.

4. Place the wheat bread on top of the three fish.

5. Place a paper towel on the sandwich. Set several heavy books on top. Leave the books on the sandwich for two days.

6. Remove the books and paper towel. Cut the sandwich in half. Observe the sandwich. How has it changed?

DIGGING DEEPER

In this project, the slices of bread represent layers of **sediment** that make up the ocean floor. The gummy fish represent the remains of dead plants and animals buried in the sediment. The books represent the pressure of more layers of sediment on top of the remains.

When you cut the sandwich in half, the gummy fish represent pockets of oil!

OIL WELL
IN A JAR

MATERIALS: clear jar, small rocks, plastic tubing, scissors, clay, ruler, sand, wooden skewer, bendable drinking straw, pitcher, water, food coloring, funnel, plastic container

Oil rises through layers of rock toward Earth's surface. Oil stops rising when it hits **impermeable** rock. This is called cap rock. It traps oil beneath it and creates a **reservoir**. Oil wells are drilled through cap rock. Oil rises to Earth's surface through the well!

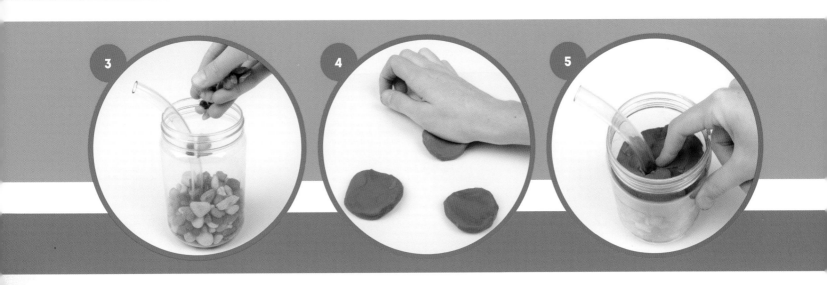

① Fill the jar about one-fourth full with small rocks.

② Cut a piece of plastic tubing a little longer than the jar is tall. Place the tubing in the jar so one end rests on the rocks.

③ Add more rocks until the jar is two-thirds full.

④ Roll several small balls of clay. Press each ball flat.

⑤ Place the pieces of clay on top of the rocks. Press the clay tightly around the tubing.

⑥ Press and spread the clay all the way to the sides of the jar. Add more clay if needed. The clay layer should be at least ¼ inch (0.6 cm) thick. The clay represents **impermeable** cap rock.

Continued on the next page.

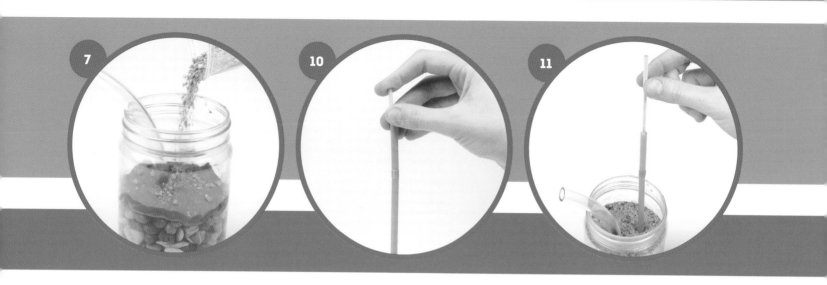

7 Add a layer of sand on top of the clay.

8 Place the wooden skewer inside the straw. The pointed end of the skewer should stick slightly out of the bottom of the straw.

9 Hold the ends of the skewer and straw together to keep the skewer in place.

10 Push the skewer and straw through the sand and clay. Stop when the end of the straw is almost at the bottom of the jar.

11 Pull the skewer out, leaving the straw in the jar. The skewer represents the drill. The straw is your oil well!

(12) Bend the top of the straw toward the outside of the jar.

(13) Fill a pitcher with water. Add several drops of food coloring. This water represents crude oil.

(14) Place the tip of the funnel in the plastic tubing.

(15) Place the jar in the plastic container. Carefully pour the water through the funnel into the jar.

(16) Observe what happens. The oil rises toward the surface of the cup. Because the oil cannot move through the cap rock, it rises up through the oil well!

CUPCAKE CORE SAMPLING

MATERIALS: white cupcake mix and ingredients, spatula, 4 bowls, food coloring, 4 spoons, foil cupcake liners, cupcake pan, oven, oven mitts, spreading knife, frosting, plastic drinking straws, paper, marker, colored pencils, sharp knife

Scientists take core samples of the rock layers around an oil well. They study the **reservoir** rock in the samples. This is rock that has spaces that hold oil. Core samples help oil drillers tell how much oil the reservoir rock holds.

core samples

prediction

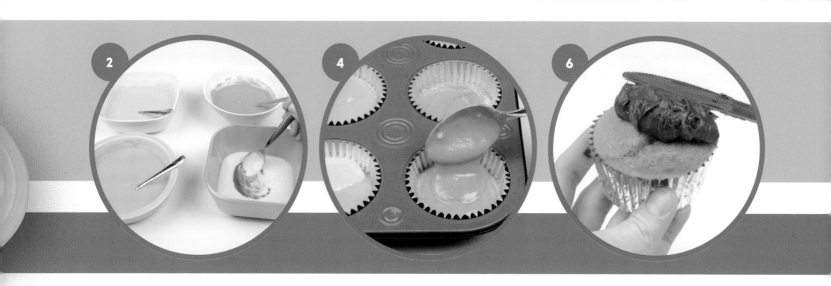

① Prepare the cupcake batter according to the instructions on the box. Divide the batter between four bowls.

② Stir two or three drops of food coloring into each bowl of batter. Use a different color for each bowl.

③ Place foil cupcake liners in the cupcake pan cups.

④ Fill each liner with at least two colors of batter. Use different color combinations and patterns to fill the liners. Do not stir the batter in the cups.

⑤ Bake the cupcakes according to the instructions on the box. Let the cupcakes cool.

⑥ Frost the cupcakes. Spread the frosting all the way to edges of the cupcakes so no cake shows.

Continued on the next page.

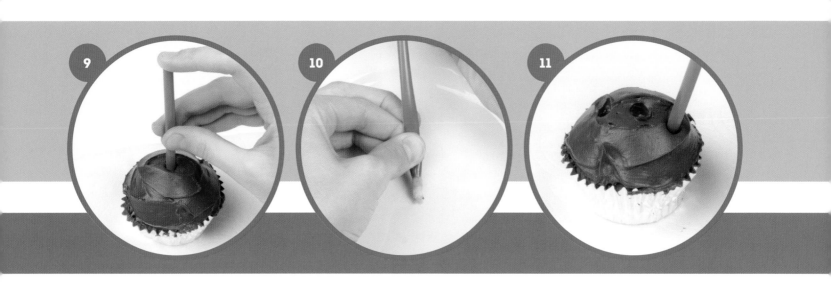

(7) The cupcake colors represent rock layers. Decide which color you want to represent **reservoir** rock.

(8) Slowly twist and push a straw into the top of a cupcake. Make sure the straw goes all the way to the bottom of the cupcake.

(9) Place your finger tightly over the top of the straw. Pull the straw out of the cupcake. Some of the cake should remain in the straw.

(10) Gently pinch the straw above the cake. Push the core sample out of the straw.

(11) Repeat steps 8 through 10 twice to take two more core samples.

12 Draw your core samples. Do they include the color that represents **reservoir** rock?

13 Based on your samples, draw what you think the **cross section** of the cupcake looks like. How much reservoir rock, if any, do you think the cupcake includes?

14 Cut the cupcake in half along the drill holes. Separate the halves and observe the cross section.

15 Compare the cross section of the cupcake to your **prediction**. How close was your guess? Is there more or less reservoir rock than you thought there would be?

OIL REFINING TOWER

MATERIALS: liquid measuring cup, honey, food coloring, spoon, clear narrow vase, corn syrup, maple syrup, whole milk, baster, water, vegetable oil, rubbing alcohol

Oil **refineries** use a special tower to separate crude oil into different fuels. Each type of fuel has a different weight. The heaviest sink to the bottom of the tower. The lightest move to the top.

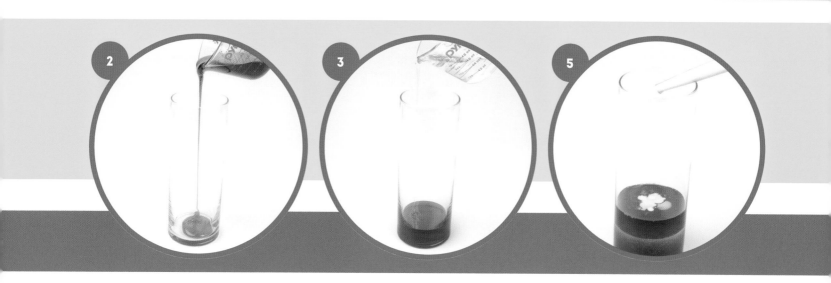

(1) Measure ½ cup of honey. Stir in a few drops of red food coloring.

(2) Pour the honey into the vase. The honey represents bitumen.

(3) Add ½ cup of corn syrup to the vase. The corn syrup represents **lubricating** oil.

(4) Add ½ cup of maple syrup to the vase. The maple syrup represents fuel oil.

(5) Measure ½ cup of whole milk. Use a baster to carefully add the milk on top of the maple syrup. The milk represents **diesel fuel**.

(6) Measure ½ cup of water. Stir in a few drops of blue food coloring.

Continued on the next page.

7 Use the baster to slowly drip the water down the side of the vase. The water represents jet fuel.

8 Measure ½ cup of vegetable oil. Use the baster to slowly drip the oil down the side of the vase. The oil represents gasoline.

9 Measure ½ cup of rubbing alcohol. Stir in a few drops of blue and red food coloring.

10 Use the baster to slowly drip the rubbing alcohol down the side of the vase. The rubbing alcohol represents liquid **petroleum** gas.

The tower used to separate fuels is called a **distillation** column. First the crude oil is heated until it boils. Then the vapors are sent into the tower. As they cool, the vapors **condense** into fuels with different weights. Each fuel is removed from the tower through its own pipe.

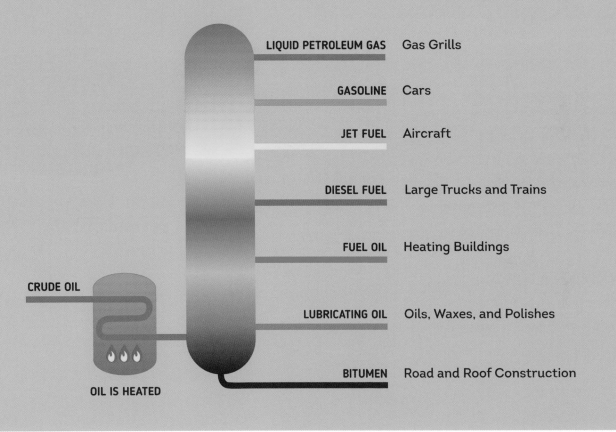

LIQUID PETROLEUM GAS	Gas Grills
GASOLINE	Cars
JET FUEL	Aircraft
DIESEL FUEL	Large Trucks and Trains
FUEL OIL	Heating Buildings
LUBRICATING OIL	Oils, Waxes, and Polishes
BITUMEN	Road and Roof Construction

CRUDE OIL

OIL IS HEATED

OIL SPILL CLEANUP

MATERIALS: measuring spoons, vegetable oil, small bowl, cocoa powder, whisk, medium bowl, water, food coloring, string, cotton balls, liquid dish soap

Offshore drilling accidents can cause oil spills in the ocean. Oil spills harm ocean plants and animals. The oil must be cleaned up as quickly as possible. There are several methods for cleaning up oil spills. Two of them are skimming and dispersion.

① Put 2 tablespoons of vegetable oil in a small bowl.

② Whisk in ½ tablespoon of cocoa powder. This mixture represents crude oil.

③ Fill a medium bowl with water. Stir in a few drops of blue food coloring.

④ Pour half the crude oil into the water. Observe how the oil and water interact.

⑤ Drag a piece of string across the top of the water to move the oil to one side of the bowl.

Continued on the next page.

6 Use cotton balls to soak up the collected oil. This is the skimming method.

7 Dump the liquid out of the medium bowl. Rinse the bowl.

8 Repeat steps 3 and 4 to make a new oil spill.

9 Add 1 teaspoon of liquid dish soap to the oil spill.

10 Use a whisk to create movement in the water. This creates the effect of waves. Observe what happens. The dish soap should break the oil pools into tiny droplets.

11 Think about your results. How do the two cleanup methods differ?

DIGGING DEEPER

In this experiment, you practiced two methods of cleaning up oil spills. There is also a third method. This is burning the oil.

DISPERSION

The dish soap represents chemicals added to the oil. The chemicals are put in the water by planes or boats. These chemicals cause the oil to break down into tiny droplets. The droplets can then mix into the water.

SKIMMING

The string represents floating **barriers** called booms. These keep the oil in an area. The cotton balls represent skimmers that remove the oil from the surface of the water.

BURNING

Before burning the oil, booms are used to hold it in place. Then the oil is set on fire and burned off the water.

CONCLUSION

Oil energy comes from burning fuels made from crude oil, These fuels power cars and are used to produce heat and electricity. However, using oil energy creates pollution. Experts are working on other energy **resources**.

QUIZ

1. New oil forms very quickly. **TRUE OR FALSE?**

2. What kind of boats carry oil?

3. What did Edwin Drake build in Titusville, Pennsylvania?

LEARN MORE ABOUT IT!

You can find out more about oil energy at the library. Or you can ask an adult to help you **research** oil energy on the internet!

Answers: 1. False 2. Oil tankers 3. Oil well

GLOSSARY

barrier – something that blocks the way, such as a fence or wall.

condense – to change from a gas into a liquid or a solid.

cross section – a view showing what the inside of something looks like after a cut has been made through it.

diesel fuel – a heavy oil used as fuel in diesel engines.

distillation – the process of heating a liquid until it gives off a gas and then cooling the gas until it becomes liquid.

fossil fuel – a fuel formed in Earth from the remains of plants or animals. Coal, oil, and natural gas are fossil fuels.

greenhouse gas – a gas, such as carbon dioxide, that traps heat in Earth's atmosphere.

impermeable – not allowing something, such as a liquid, to pass through.

lubricate – to make smooth or slippery.

petroleum – related to crude oil removed from under Earth's surface.

prediction – a statement about what will happen or might happen in the future.

refinery – a place where unwanted parts of something are removed to make it usable or valuable.

research – to find out more about something.

reservoir – a place where something is stored.

resource – something that is usable or valuable.

sediment – matter, such as rocks and sand, that is deposited by water, wind, or glaciers.